UNDERCLASS

THE PROGRAM
AND
DEATH PANEL
INCLUDED

BY S. E. MCKENZIE

DEDICATION
To everyone who has been left out in the cold

THIS BOOK IS A BOOK OF SPECULATIVE FICTION
Characters, companies, governments, places, events, are either products of the author's imagination or used fictitiously. Any resemblance to persons (living or dead), companies, governments, places and/or events, is a coincidence and unintentional.

TABLE OF CONTENTS

UNDERCLASS

S.E. McKENZIE

UNDERCLASS
I

Personal Space; Saving Grace;
Opportunity to reach potential;
Where positive direction is essential.

Stuck under the overpass,
They say they hate
Her Face;

Without make-up;
Nouveau Gestapo made up;
After he was paid up.

Question this circle?
Why would they?
They count their cash

Every Pay Day.
"We fight for dignity,"
He said

"We don't fight back"
He said.
"Non-Violence fills them with dread,"

UNDERCLASS: The Program and Death Panel Included

He said.
We will be more than a colony
In waiting.

Nouveau Gestapo said;
"Though I was busy dating;
The bait is set;

We will grow a penal colony
Over your head;
We will stay supreme

Until you scream
Somewhere all alone;
Until you submit;

Until you atone."

II
Never had a car;
Don't have a telephone;
We live under the overpass;

We live there all alone;

We awake with our hearts pounding;
For the surrounding beauty
Is astounding.

We are on the move
When the mob
Scares us to bits;

They ask the girls to show their…

We sit in the Library
Hoping for relaxation
Sharing a bit of civilization.

Nouveau Gestapo
Is on his beat
Tells us to get back onto our feet;

Out of cash; we are the new underclass;
Never bought gas
Now we must go back

To the overpass.

UNDERCLASS: The Program and Death Panel Included

We are just the residential underclass
Hoping for peace of mind
Never reaching our potential

We will never be loved
We are inconsequential;
Looking for someone kind

In a dead end town of the willfully blind.

II

There was no clue,
Or so they said,
When they found her severed head.

The shock was great;
Filled us with hate;
First responders were there too late.

The passers-by said they had no phone;
We didn't believe them
We felt so alone.

The passers-by looked at me
Then looked away;
There was nothing they would say;

Though now I know; the rumor
That framed me;
Began that way;

And no one could bring Emilee

Back to me.
For Emilee
Was now free

Though I never would be.

No longer a member
Of the residential underclass;
No longer stuck under the overpass

Now I was in cage for the rest of my days.

III

No one heard her scream
But me;
For I was hiding.

I had no phone; I was all alone;
And I could not see.
I was frozen in fear

UNDERCLASS: The Program and Death Panel Included

Though I could hear
Heavy footsteps
Above my head.

After the final scream
I knew Emilee was dead.
And that was the time

When something
Inside me
Had broken open;

To a new force
Which had just awoken.
As rumors were spun

I was also a victim of what he had done.

IV
First responders Jethro and Bill
Were having a barbecue
With a senator on the hill.

They only came by
To do their job;
Write out a form;

And do the norm;
Bill threw a flower
On the wooden box

Where Emilee lay;
There was not much to say;
Though her memory

Would never fade away;
Even to this day
I see the haunted look

Left on Emilee's severed face.

V

Though Jethro and Bill were very late
They offered no explanation
For we were the last

Of the forgotten generation;
Senator Puffy
Stayed on the hill;

UNDERCLASS: The Program and Death Panel Included

While Jethro and Bill
Pondered the meaning
Of every invoice

They had to see
Before they examined Emilee;
Then they asked me

If I knew who the suspect was;
For Emilee had no voice
Never had a choice

Before she lost her life
On that fateful night
Under the overpass.

Jethro and Bill
Said that the suspect
Was me.

They asked me why
I didn't respond
Since I was there;

S.E. McKENZIE

They asked me why I didn't care;
They threw projection after projection
At me until I wanted to scream;

For I was a residential underclass;
In a system now old and demented;
They knew I had never consented

To have everything I said
Used against me
Until the day I was dead.

Jethro and Bill
Demonized,
Marginalized,

And then socialized
With the senator on the hill
Who was shredding

Invoice after invoice;
It sounded like a thrill.
Jethro and Bill

Turned my world upside down;
The glass ceiling is now the floor;
Never had a chance;

UNDERCLASS: The Program and Death Panel Included

Turned my world upside down;
The glass ceiling is now the floor;
Never had a chance;

Just like before.

And to this day
I have not been free;
For the deeds of that night

Done by someone who wasn't me;
Jethro and Bill
Always asked who else could it be?

In less than an hour I was processed
And doomed;
While Emilee's killer

Roamed free
Waiting
To pounce
Under the overpass;

Where everything is out of sight.
If you get too close
You won't survive the night.

THE END

S.E. McKENZIE

PROGRAM

THE PROGRAM

I

Whisper, whisper, whisper;
With deadly force;
Whisper, whisper, whisper;

In a shrinking world.

The liquidator
The contractor
The phony negotiator.

Whisper, whisper, whisper;
Trip em up
So we can watch

Rip em up;
By Quasi Developer-Lord;
Tearing down outside wall.

Inside was home; so very small;
While the other side
Was tattered and torn.

In a shrinking world.

Continual gong show;
In la la land;
Lost the connection;

Ear phones were plugged in;
Now you have a digital wall;
For people to climb around;

Knock down;
So they don't feel so small;
In a shrinking world.

II

Do not get crushed in the rush;
For the world is not flat
And the roundness

Makes what you give
Come back
In a new form;

With a tireless drive
To survive
In the divided; shrinking world.

UNDERCLASS: The Program and Death Panel Included

Communication channels
Sometimes undervalued;
Sometimes overvalued;

Rarely understood;
How they shrink
The world around us.

While many fall on their face
With cameras all over the place,
The hardness grew.

In a shrinking world;
Whisper, whisper, whisper;
Nosy neighbor

Filled your bin with newspaper;

You get the fine
You get defined;
Whisper, whisper, whisper,

The smell of adult onset,
Is all around;
Filed on the Internet.

Whisper, whisper, whisper.

Not just any legal mafia; they own your sister.
Ego Clash, skin flash;
Everyone wants to be the man.

Whisper, whisper, whisper;
We have a deal for you.
Open economy

Until the barrier is installed;
To beautify your block;
Nouveau Gestapo declares;

No shock; the world is unfair.

Shrinking world
At your door;
Stuff is in demand

UNDERCLASS: The Program and Death Panel Included

More than ever before.

Whisper, whisper, whisper.
The liquidator;
The contractor,

The phony negotiator.
Rumor; maker; make-believe science;
Lost connection;

After they strangled you in debt;
The barrier to beautify
Glowed and gloated.

III
Soon one side
Was more bloated than the other side;
The new tyranny.

One side spends money
From the other side
Building the future

For the other side.
Inside
Shrinking world inflates false pride.

Outside; one side
Will tear it all down;
People wanting a new life,

A dime a dozen;
Lying to each other;
Killing sister and brother;

Neighbor feuding with neighbor.
Blame the poorest of all
For the fall.

In this shrinking world.

IV

Global warming;
Coast to coast
Love was still the force

Which mattered the most.
Cost; Paradise lost;
State

Adds to collapse;
Steely faced
Creating the underclass;

UNDERCLASS: The Program and Death Panel Included

Foreclosure of the overpass.

One side;
What a wonderful world;
The other side

Lost in the war.
In the forever
Shrinking world.

V

Fuel for negativity,
War on drugs.
Discrimination and lack of objectivity.

An excuse for the Fear Monger;
IT propagandist; to sell more
Government endorsed drug;

Alcohol;
Gap is natural; part of our agenda;
They say;

Takes so much time; we need overpay.

Whisper, whisper, whisper;
Secret society projects agenda;
Money driven segregation;

Knocks you down.

Shrinking world
Owned by a few;
Dehumanized by greed

Stigmatized by need;
With no reflection;
Too easy to strike back.

When no one sheds a tear
For your innocence lost
Knows no opportunity cost.

While looking at you with fear
Creates a feeling
That reflects; projects;

Negative energy
Of illusion
Whatever you think or feel

UNDERCLASS: The Program and Death Panel Included

Will be called delusion.
If you don't kneel to the carrot-stick god;
You could lose your way in confusion.

VI
What a night to remember
A night of purpose
A night of contradiction.

Fate,
A prison state;
That cannot change.

Said the steely faced
Gun totting
One industry town man;

Only growth industry
Was Social disorder
And exporting soldiers

To foreign places
In the shrinking world;
To kill unknown faces

For it was fate's call.
To control a world
Growing so small.

Or so they said.
To know yourself before the fall;
Was the greatest challenge of all.

You must listen to the voice
Create options; a choice;
The thinking brain In your head.

The unified voice;
One voice
Thought process

To avoid
The system
Designed to regress

UNDERCLASS: The Program and Death Panel Included

Those not controlling
The process.
Overpriced schools,

Leaving many as fools.
Imprisoned in their own mental torture
Chamber;

Trust was buried
In wasted Paradise;
The psyche-soul was now as cold as ice.

Personal freedom
Was impossible
Without financial freedom;

In the shrinking world;
Devalued currency;
Never to be free;

Would now cost more.
We all knew the lie.
You could count the days

Until you died
Of Starvation.
No crueler fate

Too late; nothing on your plate;
Some hope for power;
So they can change the state

Of hate.

Cold and steely
Fake lover
Who turned away;

Not the right religion;
Not in the right circle;
As death came too soon.

THE END

DEATH PANEL

DEATH PANEL

I

Who burnt those people
A long time ago?
Who processed the young

Before they had a chance to grow?

II

In a time called zero
The weaponized; the mechanized;
Took what they could

From the faint hearted;
Now departed;
Changed the time

But not the clock
On the wall.
Tic Toc;

Sue's heart beats to its own drummer;
Isolated Sue
Before her fall.

UNDERCLASS: The Program and Death Panel Included

III
Sue screamed out in pain;
Doctor Joe Inc. called her insane;
He said Sue looked quite odd

And disconnected from it all.
Nowhere to live
Her clothes were way too big

Was not concerned about her presentation
Could not afford representation
Perfect specimen for experimentation.

IV
Members meet in a room
Which is dark and full of gloom.
Energy vampires

Push and shove
The Broken People.
Convenience sells;

Self-serving Death Panels;

S.E. McKENZIE

Complaint driven
By the Busy Body of the day;
Craving to be Ghetto Queen;

She speculates
To elevate her own social position
While sucking in others to spin

Within her endless negative loop;

Fear mongering and gossiping
Are her tools;
When she is denied

She makes her victims
Look like fools; and we knew
Truth was the enemy of Bias;

While we tried to avoid
The adversary process;
Which the Death Panel projected

Into their Processing Room.

UNDERCLASS: The Program and Death Panel Included

While standing on the street corner
Busy Body speculates
Sometimes cruelly;

Elevates her standing;
As Ghetto Queen; Her only way;
To feel important;

For time will soon make
Busy Body obsolete.
Even though she craves to be elite.

Standing by the needle exchange
Ghetto Queen shouts insults
At Sue walking home

All alone in the Negative Zone;
Where the negativity is draining;
Not much effort goes to sustaining

Positivity dies too quickly.

V

Sue must play along
Pretend that Joe Inc. is right
Even when he is wrong;

Pretend all night;
Pretend until the morning light
Arrives to bring in a new day

Not yet touched
By the Death Panel
Trying to find a way

To fit Sue's case into the billing code.

VI

Social service;
With no social mobility;
Setting Sue up for lower society;

Dr. Joe Inc. complained about Sue's smell;
Dr. Joe Inc. said Sue looked like hell;
Dr. Joe Inc. would micro-manage

Sue as if she were a beast.

UNDERCLASS: The Program and Death Panel Included

Dr. Joe Inc.; the micro-aggressor;
Creating; positioning;
Reinforcing a lower social order;

For profit;
As predator;
On Sue's psyche, Dr. Joe Inc. would feast.

Death Panel;
They meet
Without having to greet

Sue trying to prove a negative;
Risk to sanity; consultation
Can be done over the phone

With someone above
In the social pecking order;
No mentor just micro-aggressor;

No social security lawyer
Found in the telephone book;
Go screaming down the street;

And the moneyed criminal lawyers
Will give Sue another look;
The police will help them book;

While we knew the crime.

Money driven; complaint driven;
Creating a lower social position;
Less competition;

Without social mobility
How can anyone be free?
Micro aggressor

Picks a fight
Causes a fright
And entry into a lower social order.

Death panels stay on call;
For convenience sake.
Writing off Sue but could be you;

Poverty legislated;
Position dictated;
With no way out.

UNDERCLASS: The Program and Death Panel Included

Blocking entry
Blocking integration
For a new generation

Without a title.

Creating artificial structure
A disadvantage for one
Is an advantage for another;

Social predator;
Gave Sue a glass of wine at work
Then complained to the higher up

That Sue was drinking at work;
The Nouveau Gestapo was called
And processed Sue that very day;

Never to be unmarked again;
Precious lover never answering her call;
Steely silence made Sue scream;

Not the right religion
Not in the right circle
Isolation; never selected

Now positioned to be neglected;

Was not seen as a mistake.
Manufactured cause to discriminate
It was money driven;

It was complaint driven;
No complaint was too small;
The micro-managers; the micro-aggressors

Now had a full time job making Sue crawl.

And no money could be made
In social security law;
So Sue was treated like a criminal instead.

Made the fear worse in Sue's head;
In a world where every door
Was now shut in her face day after day;

Often a victim of Ghetto Queen's hysteria
Whenever seen
In a public area.

UNDERCLASS: The Program and Death Panel Included

Year after year;
Personal comment
Manufactured consent.

Though there was no smell of alcohol
The Nouveau Gestapo would answer the call
If Sue was labeled alcoholic;

For the new war was not just economic;

In the red-lined district
Where Government sponsored beer
Was always near; a better chance to succeed in business

If you drink with the right people;
Sell to the right people
Complain to the right people.

And a long time ago the busy body of the day
The Ghetto Queen, wanted Sue to go away;
And offered her a drink

Then waved a letter in her face,
Accused her of sending it to her place,
In front of everyone in the room

Sue was mortified
And wished that she had died.
Wondered why someone she admired would lie.

Busy Body then phoned
The Nouveau Gestapo
With her complaint

While Sue was still in shock feeling faint.

From that day on Sue was never the same;
Busy Body said Sue was caught drinking at work;
While Busy Body looked out of the window

Always ready to complain
Whenever Sue was near;
Filled Sue with Fear;

Phoned her friends
Who were always near
And they all put Sue on their list;

To watch;

They were certain that Sue
Was a descendant from
Witches due to her nose

UNDERCLASS: The Program and Death Panel Included

Due to her clothes;
The micro-aggressor
Told the under class

Where to sit
And where to stand
And whenever she stared at Sue

She felt fear, she said;
Did not know
What to do, she said.

Phoned the Nouveau Gestapo
To take Sue away;
The vulture cultures were on their way.

Even though Sue just lived down our street
She was not treated like a neighbor
By the wanna-be elite.

Poor Sue;
What could she do:
Now victim of self-fulfilling prophecy

Very few would let her be.

VII

How can anyone be free
In a multi-tier society;
Secret Currency is paid on entry

To Secret Watcher-Society.

We said Sue had the right to live
And society needed to shift
In order to give Sue a lift.

A Two-way gift; growing to be
The best
She could be.

Doctor Joe Inc. disagreed;
And on these cases
He did feed;

Never considered
How self-fulfilling prophecies
Created the gap; created the need;

UNDERCLASS: The Program and Death Panel Included

Sue went to a Human Rights Channel;
And they took her case
But Dr. Joe Inc.'s word was believed

As soon as they saw Sue's face.
The Channel had a robot investigator
Listened to what Dr. Joe Inc.'s lawyers had to say

The team of lawyers
Were paid
Thousands of dollars a day

To make the Human Rights Channel go away;
Took out the rule that disallowed
The Human rights Tribunal to make a phone call.

And they said
Sue's fear
Was just in her head.

Hypocrisy;

S.E. McKENZIE

VIII

Money was being made
In a war
To prevent World War III

So the King of Bling said;
Out of this world context;
Bias was innocent, so they said;

False Pride;
Arrogant killer;
King of Bling

The Divine Thriller;
Able to turn
Blood into wine.

IX

We were drafted to fight a war
To prevent a war.
Across the sea;

It was said
They were fighting
For human rights;

UNDERCLASS: The Program and Death Panel Included

So everyone was dressed to kill;
Conflict of interest;
Multiple roles for financial gain.

X

Sometimes Sue screams out in pain
But then the pain
Goes away when she remembers

Her lover from days gone by;

And life goes on
Expensively;
And soon Sue will no longer be.

The way she used to be.

For now Sue has a label hanging
From her big toe;
And nothing more we shall know.

Death Panel;
They count all the food
That Sue won't have to eat.

They don't count
The past contribution
And Sue's own interest compounding;

The heartlessness was astounding.

Death Panel;
They will sell the shoes
Off Sue's feet;

Death panel;
Domain of the elite
Finding a way to fit their desired outcome

Into the Billing Code.

Profit for the shareholders;
Less expense for the taxpayers
Death Panel;

Needed to fit the billing code
In a civilized way
So everyone waves

As sue passes away.
Death Panel remains
Disengaged;

Silently; humanity was estranged;
Never speaking to her;
Just at her;

UNDERCLASS: The Program and Death Panel Included

Never answering her call;
Always making her feel small;
In a world of plenty

They were so many
Moving along
On empty.

Moving mountains
Made from mole hills
Micro-aggression; macro-suggestion;

"Don't say
That one day
The billing code will finance

Paid killers;
Don't say the Truth;
In polite society that is rude;

Don't use words like Death that are so crude."

Ordered the King of Bling;
"Pray for power or anything
But the truth;

For Truth is the enemy of Bias."

Death greets Sue at the door
Gone from life
For evermore.

Sue no longer will exist;
Sue will never be missed;
Or so the Death Panel will say.

World around the mirror;
The world so small;
And getting meaner;

Day by day
The Death Panel
Will shape the way.

Day by day
They find a way
To keep it clean;

UNDERCLASS: The Program and Death Panel Included

They smile
When they tell you how to live
And tell you when to die.

Billing Code
The new bible
In the world where war makers

Say they crave peace;
There is no plan
In the design to make change.

Just dollars;
Weaponized; mechanized;
Bureaucracy;

Using the young for cannon fodder.

Contradicting what you experience;
Sheltered on the other side;
Of the glass ceiling;

Just a feeling
Micro-aggressor
Micro-manager

No right of way for Sue.

So smothering;
For Sue
Could no longer scream;

The outcome
Was not measured
For the secret process was not yet covered

Under the billing code.

THE END

Produced by S.E. McKenzie Productions
First Print Edition June 2015

Enquiries: 1(778)992-2453
Mailing Address:
S. E. McKenzie Productions
168 B 5th St.
Courtenay, BC
V9N 1J4

Email Address:
messidartha@aol.com

http://www.amazon.com/SarahMcKenzie/e/B00H9RWX48/